Houghton
Mifflin
Harcourt

MATH Expressions
Common Core

Dr. Karen C. Fuson

GRADE

1

Volume 2

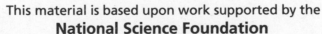

This material is based upon work supported by the
National Science Foundation
under Grant Numbers
ESI-9816320, REC-9806020, and RED-935373.

Any opinions, findings, and conclusions, or recommendations expressed in this material
are those of the author and do not necessarily reflect the views of the National Science Foundation.

VOLUME 2 CONTENTS

UNIT 5 Place Value Situations

VOLUME 2 CONTENTS *(continued)*

UNIT 6 Comparisons and Data

UNIT 7 Geometry, Measurement, and Equal Shares

* This lesson consists only of activities from the Teacher Edition.

© Houghton Mifflin Harcourt Publishing Company

© Houghton Mifflin Harcourt Publishing Company

UNIT 8 Two-Digit Addition

BIG IDEA	Add 2-Digit Numbers

Student Resources

* This lesson consists only of activities from the Teacher Edition.

Family Letter

Dear Family:

In the previous unit, your child learned the Make a Ten strategy to find teen totals. Now, your child builds on previous knowledge to use make a ten to find an unknown partner. The Make a Ten strategy is explained below.

In a teen addition problem such as 9 + 5, children break apart the lesser number to make a ten with the greater number. Because 9 + 1 = 10, they break apart 5 into 1 + 4. Then they add the extra 4 onto 10 to find the total. A similar method is used to find unknown partners with teen totals. Children look for ways to make a ten because it is easier to add onto 10.

In the *Math Expressions* program, Make-a-Ten Cards help children use this method. Each card has a problem on the front. The back shows the answer and illustrates the Make a Ten strategy using pictures of dots. Below the pictures are corresponding numbers to help children understand how to make a ten. Practice the method with your child. As you continue to practice the Make a Ten strategy with your child, your child will become more adept at using mental math.

If you have any question about the Make a Ten strategy, please contact me.

Sincerely,
Your child's teacher

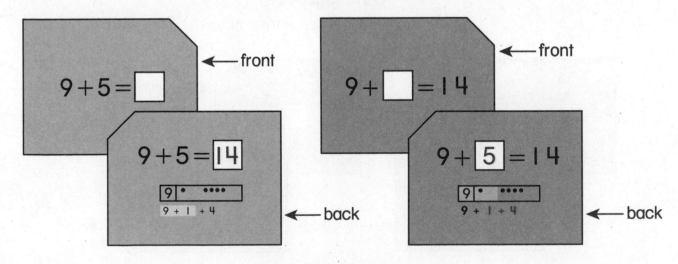

Make-a-Ten Cards

COMMON CORE

Unit 5 includes the Common Core Standards for Mathematical Content for Operations and Algebraic Thinking 1.OA.1, 1.OA.2, 1.OA.3, 1.OA.4, 1.OA.5, 1.OA.6, 1.OA.8; Number and Operations in Base Ten, 1.NBT.1, 1.NBT.2, 1.NBT.2c, 1.NBT.4, 1.NBT.5, 1.NBT.6 and all Mathematical Practices.

Estimada familia:

En la unidad anterior, su niño aprendió la Estrategia hacer decenas para hallar totales de números de 11 a 19. Ahora, su niño ampliará esos conocimientos previos y hará decenas para hallar una parte desconocida. La Estrategia hacer decenas se explica debajo.

En una suma con números de 11 a 19, tal como 9 + 5, los niños separan el número menor para formar una decena con el número mayor. Como 9 + 1 = 10, separan el 5 en 1 + 4. Luego suman al 10 los 4 que sobran para hallar el total. Un método semejante se usa para hallar partes desconocidas con totales de números de 11 a 19. Los niños buscan maneras de formar una decena porque es más fácil sumar con 10.

En el programa *Math Expressions* las tarjetas de hacer decenas ayudan a los niños a usar este método. Cada tarjeta tiene un problema en el frente. En el reverso se muestra la respuesta y se ilustra la Estrategia hacer decenas mediante dibujos de puntos. Debajo de los dibujos están los números correspondientes para ayudar a los niños a comprender cómo se hace una decena. Practique el método con su niño. A medida que practican la estrategia, su niño adquirirá mayor dominio del cálculo mental.

Si tiene alguna pregunta sobre la Estrategia hacer decenas, por favor comuníquese conmigo.

Atentamente,
El maestro de su niño

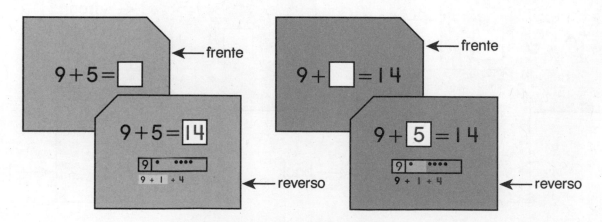

Tarjetas de hacer decenas

COMMON
CORE

La Unidad 5 incluye los Common Core Standards for Mathematical Content for Operations and Algebraic Thinking 1.OA.1, 1.OA.2, 1.OA.3, 1.OA.4, 1.OA.5, 1.OA.6, 1.OA.8; Number and Operations in Base Ten, 1.NBT.1, 1.NBT.2, 1.NBT.2c, 1.NBT.4, 1.NBT.5, 1.NBT.6 and all Mathematical Practices.

$7 + \boxed{} = 16$ $6 + \boxed{} = 15$ $7 + \boxed{} = 11$

$8 + \boxed{} = 12$ $9 + \boxed{} = 13$ $6 + \boxed{} = 11$

$7 + \boxed{} = 12$ $8 + \boxed{} = 13$ $9 + \boxed{} = 14$

$5 + \boxed{} = 11$ $9 + \boxed{} = 18$ $7 + \boxed{} = 13$

$8 + \boxed{} = 14$ $9 + \boxed{} = 15$ $4 + \boxed{} = 11$

$7 + \boxed{4} = 11$

7 | ••• •
7 + 3 + 1

$6 + \boxed{9} = 15$

6 | •••• •••••
6 + 4 + 5

$7 + \boxed{9} = 16$

7 | ••• •••
      •••
7 + 3 + 6

$6 + \boxed{5} = 11$

6 | •••• •
6 + 4 + 1

$9 + \boxed{4} = 13$

9 | • •••
9 + 1 + 3

$8 + \boxed{4} = 12$

8 | •• ••
8 + 2 + 2

$9 + \boxed{5} = 14$

9 | • ••••
9 + 1 + 4

$8 + \boxed{5} = 13$

8 | •• •••
8 + 2 + 3

$7 + \boxed{5} = 12$

7 | ••• ••
7 + 3 + 2

$7 + \boxed{6} = 13$

7 | ••• •••
7 + 3 + 3

$9 + \boxed{9} = 18$

9 | • •••••
      •••
9 + 1 + 8

$5 + \boxed{6} = 11$

5 | ••••• •
5 + 5 + 1

$4 + \boxed{7} = 11$

4 | ••••• •
4 + 6 + 1

$9 + \boxed{6} = 15$

9 | • •••••
9 + 1 + 5

$8 + \boxed{6} = 14$

8 | •• ••••
8 + 2 + 4

Purple Make-a-Ten Cards

$5 + \boxed{} = 12$	$6 + \boxed{} = 13$	$8 + \boxed{} = 17$
$8 + \boxed{} = 15$	$9 + \boxed{} = 16$	$3 + \boxed{} = 11$
$4 + \boxed{} = 12$	$5 + \boxed{} = 13$	$6 + \boxed{} = 14$
$7 + \boxed{} = 15$	$8 + \boxed{} = 16$	$9 + \boxed{} = 17$
$3 + \boxed{} = 12$	$4 + \boxed{} = 13$	$5 + \boxed{} = 14$

$8 + \boxed{9} = 17$

8 | •• | •••••
8 + 2 + 7

$6 + \boxed{7} = 13$

6 | •••• | •••
6 + 4 + 3

$5 + \boxed{7} = 12$

5 | ••••• | ••
5 + 5 + 2

$3 + \boxed{8} = 11$

3 | ••••••• | •
3 + 7 + 1

$9 + \boxed{7} = 16$

9 | • | •••••
9 + 1 + 6

$8 + \boxed{7} = 15$

8 | •• | •••••
8 + 2 + 5

$6 + \boxed{8} = 14$

6 | •••• | ••••
6 + 4 + 4

$5 + \boxed{8} = 13$

5 | ••••• | •••
5 + 5 + 3

$4 + \boxed{8} = 12$

4 | •••••• | ••
4 + 6 + 2

$9 + \boxed{8} = 17$

9 | • | •••••••
9 + 1 + 7

$8 + \boxed{8} = 16$

8 | •• | ••••••
8 + 2 + 6

$7 + \boxed{8} = 15$

7 | ••• | •••••
7 + 3 + 5

$5 + \boxed{9} = 14$

5 | ••••• | ••••
5 + 5 + 4

$4 + \boxed{9} = 13$

4 | •••••• | •••
4 + 6 + 3

$3 + \boxed{9} = 12$

3 | ••••••• | ••
3 + 7 + 2

Purple Make-a-Ten Cards

Name _____

VOCABULARY
unknown partner

Match the equation with the picture that shows
how to use the Make a Ten strategy to solve.
Write the **unknown partner**.

1. $8 +$ ☐ $= 12$

2. $9 +$ ☐ $= 15$

3. $7 +$ ☐ $= 12$

4. $8 +$ ☐ $= 14$

5. $9 +$ ☐ $= 12$

6. $8 +$ ☐ $= 15$

7. $9 +$ ☐ $= 11$

8. $9 +$ ☐ $= 17$

9. $7 +$ ☐ $= 11$

9	• • •
7	• • • • •
9	• •
8	• • • •
8	• • • • • •
9	• • • • • •
9	• • • • • • • •
8	• • • • • • •
7	• • • •

Solve the story problem.

Show your work. Use drawings, numbers, or words.

---

10. Some birds are in a tree. 5 more birds fly into the tree. Now there are 13 birds. How many birds were in the tree before?

tree

[ ] _____
    label

---

11. 14 cats are black or white. 8 cats are black. How many cats are white?

cat

[ ] _____
    label

---

12. 10 kites are big. 10 kites are small. How many kites are there?

kite

[ ] _____
    label

---

13. Juan has 8 books. Meg brings more books. Now there are 17 books. How many books does Meg bring?

book

[ ] _____
    label

$15 - 6 = \boxed{}$ $16 - 7 = \boxed{}$ $11 - 7 = \boxed{}$

$12 - 8 = \boxed{}$ $13 - 9 = \boxed{}$ $11 - 6 = \boxed{}$

$12 - 7 = \boxed{}$ $13 - 8 = \boxed{}$ $14 - 9 = \boxed{}$

$11 - 5 = \boxed{}$ $17 - 8 = \boxed{}$ $13 - 7 = \boxed{}$

$14 - 8 = \boxed{}$ $15 - 9 = \boxed{}$ $11 - 4 = \boxed{}$

$11 - 7 = \boxed{4}$

| 7 | ••• | • |

$7 + 3 + 1$

$16 - 7 = \boxed{9}$

| 7 | ••• | ••••• |

$7 + 3 + 6$

$15 - 6 = \boxed{9}$

| 6 | •••• | ••••• |

$6 + 4 + 5$

$11 - 6 = \boxed{5}$

| 6 | •••• | • |

$6 + 4 + 1$

$13 - 9 = \boxed{4}$

| 9 | • | ••• |

$9 + 1 + 3$

$12 - 8 = \boxed{4}$

| 8 | •• | •• |

$8 + 2 + 2$

$14 - 9 = \boxed{5}$

| 9 | • | •••• |

$9 + 1 + 4$

$13 - 8 = \boxed{5}$

| 8 | •• | ••• |

$8 + 2 + 3$

$12 - 7 = \boxed{5}$

| 7 | ••• | •• |

$7 + 3 + 2$

$13 - 7 = \boxed{6}$

| 7 | ••• | ••• |

$7 + 3 + 3$

$17 - 8 = \boxed{9}$

| 8 | •• | ••••• |

$8 + 2 + 7$

$11 - 5 = \boxed{6}$

| 5 | ••••• | • |

$5 + 5 + 1$

$11 - 4 = \boxed{7}$

| 4 | •••• | • |

$4 + 6 + 1$

$15 - 9 = \boxed{6}$

| 9 | • | ••••• |

$9 + 1 + 5$

$14 - 8 = \boxed{6}$

| 8 | •• | •••• |

$8 + 2 + 4$

Blue Make-a-Ten Cards

$12 - 5 = \boxed{}$

$13 - 6 = \boxed{}$

$18 - 9 = \boxed{}$

$15 - 8 = \boxed{}$

$16 - 9 = \boxed{}$

$11 - 3 = \boxed{}$

$12 - 4 = \boxed{}$

$13 - 5 = \boxed{}$

$14 - 6 = \boxed{}$

$15 - 7 = \boxed{}$

$16 - 8 = \boxed{}$

$17 - 9 = \boxed{}$

$12 - 3 = \boxed{}$

$13 - 4 = \boxed{}$

$14 - 5 = \boxed{}$

$18 - 9 = \boxed{9}$

$9 + 1 + 8$

$13 - 6 = \boxed{7}$

$6 + 4 + 3$

$12 - 5 = \boxed{7}$

$5 + 5 + 2$

$11 - 3 = \boxed{8}$

$3 + 7 + 1$

$16 - 9 = \boxed{7}$

$9 + 1 + 6$

$15 - 8 = \boxed{7}$

$8 + 2 + 5$

$14 - 6 = \boxed{8}$

$6 + 4 + 4$

$13 - 5 = \boxed{8}$

$5 + 5 + 3$

$12 - 4 = \boxed{8}$

$4 + 6 + 2$

$17 - 9 = \boxed{8}$

$9 + 1 + 7$

$16 - 8 = \boxed{8}$

$8 + 2 + 6$

$15 - 7 = \boxed{8}$

$7 + 3 + 5$

$14 - 5 = \boxed{9}$

$5 + 5 + 4$

$13 - 4 = \boxed{9}$

$4 + 6 + 3$

$12 - 3 = \boxed{9}$

$3 + 7 + 2$

Blue Make-a-Ten Cards

Name

Match the equation with the picture that shows how to use the Make a Ten strategy to solve.

1. $12 - 8 = \boxed{}$

7	• • • • • •

2. $14 - 9 = \boxed{}$

8	• • • • • •

3. $13 - 7 = \boxed{}$

8	• • • •

4. $15 - 8 = \boxed{}$

7	• • • • •

5. $14 - 8 = \boxed{}$

9	• • • • •

6. $12 - 7 = \boxed{}$

6	• • • • • • • •

7. $11 - 8 = \boxed{}$

8	• • • • • • •

8. $14 - 6 = \boxed{}$

9	• •

9. $11 - 9 = \boxed{}$

8	• • •

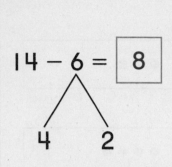

	Step 1	Step 2
$14 - 6 = \boxed{8}$	$14 - 4 = 10$	$10 - 2 = 8$

Subtract.

10. $15 - 8 = \boxed{}$

11. $13 - 4 = \boxed{}$

12. $12 - 9 = \boxed{}$

13. $17 - 9 = \boxed{}$

Solve the story problem.

Show your work. Use drawings, numbers, or words.

1. 17 berries are in a bowl. 9 are red and the rest are purple. How many berries are purple?

bowl

☐ _____
label

2. I draw some stars. 8 are large and 7 are small. How many stars do I draw?

star

☐ _____
label

3. There are 14 puppies. Some are brown and some are black. How many brown and black puppies could there be?
Show three answers.

puppy

☐ brown puppies and ☐ black puppies

or ☐ brown puppies and ☐ black puppies

or ☐ brown puppies and ☐ black puppies

Solve the story problem.

4. 15 frogs are by the pond. 9 hop away. How many frogs are there now?

pond

☐ _____
    label

5. 16 butterflies are in the garden. Some fly away. There are 8 left. How many butterflies fly away?

butterflies

☐ _____
    label

6. Some grapes are in a bowl. I eat 6 of them. Now there are 7 grapes. How many grapes were in the bowl before?

grapes

☐ _____
    label

7. There are 12 horses in a field. Some run away. Now there are 5 horses. How many horses run away?

horse

☐ _____
    label

Match the equation with the picture that shows
how to use the Make a Ten strategy to solve.

1. 8 + ☐ = 14

| 8 | •• • |

2. 7 + 5 = ☐

| 6 | ••••• ••••• |

3. 8 + 3 = ☐

| 8 | •• •••• • |

4. 6 + ☐ = 15

| 7 | ••• ••• |

5. 9 + ☐ = 18

| 9 | • ••••• |

6. 9 + ☐ = 15

| 8 | •• •• |

7. 8 + 4 = ☐

| 9 | • ••••••••• |

8. 7 + 6 = ☐

| 7 | ••• •• |

9. Ring the picture above that shows
how to use the Make a Ten strategy
to solve the equation.

13 − 7 = ☐

Add.

10. $9 + 3 =$ ☐   11. $7 + 8 =$ ☐   12. $7 + 5 =$ ☐

13. $10 + 10 =$ ☐   14. $8 + 5 =$ ☐   15. $2 + 9 =$ ☐

16. $11 + 9 =$ ☐   17. $12 + 7 =$ ☐   18. $8 + 12 =$ ☐

Find the unknown partner.

19. $9 +$ ☐ $= 14$ 20. $10 +$ ☐ $= 19$ 21. $6 +$ ☐ $= 13$

22. ☐ $+ 4 = 12$ 23. ☐ $+ 8 = 11$ 24. ☐ $+ 6 = 15$

Subtract.

25. $11 - 2 =$ ☐   26. $14 - 6 =$ ☐   27. $13 - 9 =$ ☐

28. $16 - 8 =$ ☐   29. $13 - 7 =$ ☐   30. $12 - 5 =$ ☐

PATH to FLUENCY Subtract.

1. $10 - 8 =$ ☐   2. $7 - 1 =$ ☐   3. $6 - 6 =$ ☐

4. $9 - 7 =$ ☐   5. $8 - 4 =$ ☐   6. $10 - 6 =$ ☐

Small Group Practice with Teen Problems

1. Rosa reads 8 stories. Tim reads 5 stories.
   How many stories do they read in all?

2. Rosa reads 8 stories. Tim also reads some stories.
   They read 13 stories in all. How many stories
   does Tim read?

3. Rosa reads some stories. Tim reads 5 stories.
   They read 13 stories in all. How many stories
   does Rosa read?

Some crayons are in a box.
I take 6 crayons out.
Now there are 9 crayons in the box.
How many crayons were in the box before?

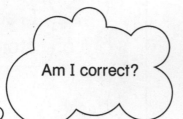

Am I correct?

4. Look at what Puzzled Penguin wrote.

| 9 | − | 6 | = | 3 |

| 3 | crayons

5. Help Puzzled Penguin.

| | − | | = | |

| | crayons

Teen Problems with Various Unknowns

Model and solve the story problem.
Color to show your model.
Cross out the cubes you do not use.

1. There are 6 red pencils, 5 yellow pencils,
and 7 green pencils in a cup.
How many pencils are in the cup?

cup

OOOOOOOOOOOOOOOOOOOO

☐ _____
label

2. I have 4 white fish, 2 black fish,
and 6 orange fish in my fish tank.
How many fish are in my fish tank?

fish

OOOOOOOOOOOOOOOOOOOO

☐ _____
label

3. There are 3 pears on the table, 10 pears
in a basket, and 7 pears in a bowl.
How many pears are there?

pear

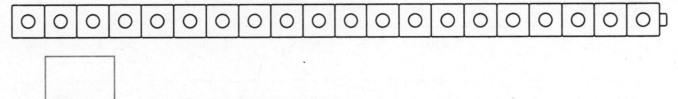

☐ _____
label

Solve the story problem.

Show your work. Use drawings, numbers, or words.

---

4. There are 5 red crayons, 9 blue crayons, and 1 yellow crayon on the table. How many crayons are on the table?

crayon

◻ _____
       label

---

5. Charlie sees 4 books on a desk, 6 books on a shelf, and 8 books on a cart. How many books does Charlie see?

desk

◻ _____
       label

---

6. Gina finds 7 seashells. Paul finds 6 seashells. Lee finds 3 seashells. How many seashells do they find altogether?

seashell

◻ _____
       label

Problems with Three Addends

VOCABULARY
10-group

1. Ring **10-groups**. Count by tens and ones.
   Write the number.

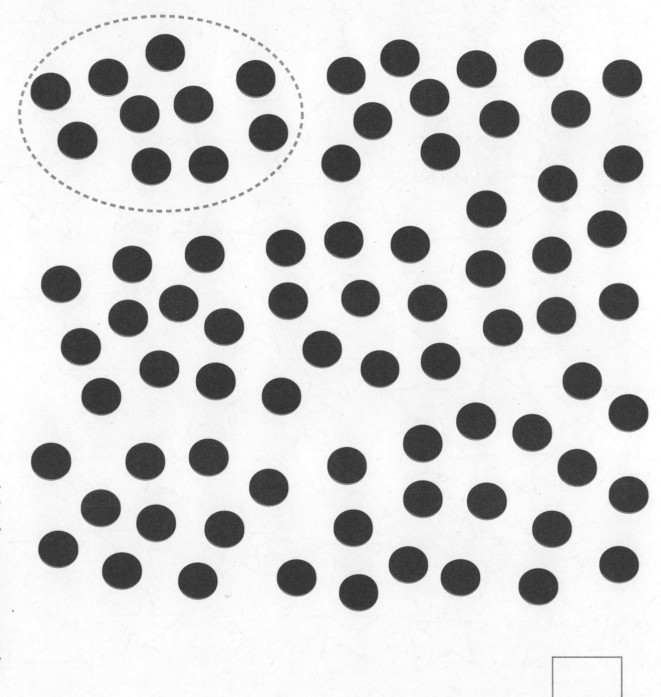

2. Color each 10-group a different color.
Count by tens and ones. Write the number.

Dear Family:

The next several lessons of this unit build upon what the class learned previously about tens and ones. The Hundred Grid is a tool that allows children to see 10-based patterns in sequence. Seeing numbers in the ordered rows and columns of the Hundred Grid helps children better understand number relationships as they:

- continue to practice with 10-groups, adding tens to any 2-digit number, with totals to 100;
- explore 2-digit subtraction, subtracting tens from decade numbers;
- connect what they know about 10-partners to now find 100-partners.

1	11	21	31	41	51	61	71	81	91
2	12	22	32	42	52	62	72	82	92
3	13	23	33	43	53	63	73	83	93
4	14	24	34	44	54	64	74	84	94
5	15	25	35	45	55	65	75	85	95
6	16	26	36	46	56	66	76	86	96
7	17	27	37	47	57	67	77	87	97
8	18	28	38	48	58	68	78	88	98
9	19	29	39	49	59	69	79	89	99
10	20	30	40	50	60	70	80	90	100

3   ○○○
13 | ○○○
23 | | ○○○
33 | | | ○○○
43 | | | | ○○○
53 | | | | | ○○○
63 | | | | | | ○○○
73 | | | | | | | ○○○
83 | | | | | | | | ○○○
93 | | | | | | | | | ○○○

If you have any questions or problems, please contact me.

Sincerely,
Your child's teacher

 COMMON CORE Unit 5 includes the Common Core Standards for Mathematical Content for Operations and Algebraic Thinking 1.OA.1, 1.OA.2, 1.OA.3, 1.OA.4, 1.OA.5, 1.OA.6, 1.OA.8; Number and Operations in Base Ten, 1.NBT.1, 1.NBT.2, 1.NBT.2c, 1.NBT.4, 1.NBT.5, 1.NBT.6 and all Mathematical Practices.

Estimada familia:

Las siguientes lecciones en esta unidad amplían lo que la clase aprendió anteriormente acerca de decenas y unidades. La Cuadrícula de 100 es un instrumento que permite observar patrones de base 10 en secuencia. Observar los números ordenados en hileras y columnas en la Cuadrícula de 100 ayudará a los niños a comprender mejor la relación entre los números mientras:

- continúan practicando con grupos de 10, sumando decenas a números de 2 dígitos con totales hasta 100;

- exploran la resta de números de 2 dígitos, restando decenas de números que terminan en cero;

- relacionan lo que saben acerca de las partes de 10 para hallar partes de 100.

1	11	21	31	41	51	61	71	81	91
2	12	22	32	42	52	62	72	82	92
3	13	23	33	43	53	63	73	83	93
4	14	24	34	44	54	64	74	84	94
5	15	25	35	45	55	65	75	85	95
6	16	26	36	46	56	66	76	86	96
7	17	27	37	47	57	67	77	87	97
8	18	28	38	48	58	68	78	88	98
9	19	29	39	49	59	69	79	89	99
10	20	30	40	50	60	70	80	90	100

3 ooo

13 | ooo

23 || ooo

33 ||| ooo

43 |||| ooo

53 ||||| ooo

63 ||||| | ooo

73 ||||| || ooo

83 ||||| ||| ooo

93 ||||| |||| ooo

Si tiene alguna pregunta o algún comentario comuníquese conmigo.

Atentamente,
El maestro de su niño

© Houghton Mifflin Harcourt Publishing Company

La Unidad 5 incluye los Common Core Standards for Mathematical Content for Operations and Algebraic Thinking 1.OA.1, 1.OA.2, 1.OA.3, 1.OA.4, 1.OA.5, 1.OA.6, 1.OA.8; Number and Operations in Base Ten, 1.NBT.1, 1.NBT.2, 1.NBT.2c, 1.NBT.4, 1.NBT.5, 1.NBT.6 and all Mathematical Practices.

VOCABULARY
column
grid

1. Write the numbers 1–120 in **columns**.

1	11										
2											
10									100		120

Use the **grid** to find 10 more. Write the number.

2. 29   **3.** 72 ⬜ **4.** 45 ⬜ **5.** 90 ⬜

Use the grid to find 10 less. Write the number.

6. 39 ⬜ **7.** 72 ⬜ **8.** 91 ⬜ **9.** 20

VOCABULARY
row

10. Write the numbers 1–120 in **rows**.

1	2								10
11									
									100
									120

Use the grid to find 10 more.
Write the number.

Use the grid to find 10 less.
Write the number.

11. 63 ☐   **12.** 51 ☐   **13.** 83 ☐   **14.** 51 ☐

Make a Hundred Grid

1. Listen to the directions.

1	11	21	31	41	51	61	71	81	91
2	12	22	32	42	52	62	72	82	92
3	13	23	33	43	53	63	73	83	93
4	14	24	34	44	54	64	74	84	94
5	15	25	35	45	55	65	75	85	95
6	16	26	36	46	56	66	76	86	96
7	17	27	37	47	57	67	77	87	97
8	18	28	38	48	58	68	78	88	98
9	19	29	39	49	59	69	79	89	99
10	20	30	40	50	60	70	80	90	100

Add tens.

2. 89 + 10 = ☐

3. 43 + 20 = ☐

4. 28 + 50 = ☐

5. 32 + 40 = ☐

6. 11 + 20 = ☐

7. 42 + 30 = ☐

8. 52 + 40 = ☐

9. 12 + 40 = ☐

10. 10 + 19 = ☐

11. 60 + 26 = ☐

Subtract tens.

12. 30 − 20 = ☐

13. 60 − 10 = ☐

14. 70 − 40 = ☐

15. 70 − 20 = ☐

16. 90 − 60 = ☐

17. 80 − 70 = ☐

18. 90 − 10 = ☐

19. 50 − 40 = ☐

Solve.

1. 80 + 20 = ☐

2. 30 + 70 = ☐

3. 10 + ☐ = 100

4. 50 + ☐ = 100

5. 100 = 20 + ☐

6. 100 = 40 + ☐

7. 20 + 50 = ☐

8. 10 + 80 = ☐

9. 0 + 60 = ☐

10. 20 + 20 = ☐

11. 40 − 40 = ☐

12. 80 − 0 = ☐

13. 70 − 60 = ☐

14. 60 − 30 = ☐

15. 60 − 10 = ☐

10 + ☐ = 60

16. 70 − 40 = ☐

40 + ☐ = 70

17. 50 − 20 = ☐

20 + ☐ = 50

18. 90 − 50 = ☐

50 + ☐ = 90

19. Look at what Puzzled Penguin wrote.

70 − 20 = | 5 |

Am I correct?

20. Help Puzzled Penguin.

70 − 20 = | |

PATH to FLUENCY **Add.**

1. 1 + 8 = | |

2. 5 + 4 = | |

3. 4 + 6 = | |

4. 4 + 2 = | |

5. 7 + 1 = | |

6. 3 + 4 = | |

PATH to FLUENCY **Subtract.**

7. 9 − 3 = | |

8. 6 − 1 = | |

9. 7 − 6 = | |

10. 8 − 6 = | |

11. 10 − 3 = | |

12. 8 − 3 = | |

▶ Math and Gardening

Use the picture.
Write the numbers to solve.

---

1. Casey helps gather fruit. How many pieces of fruit does Casey gather?

☐ 🍋 + ☐ 🫐 + ☐ 🍊 = ?

☐ + ☐ = ☐ pieces of fruit

---

2. Casey helps gather vegetables. How many vegetables does Casey gather?

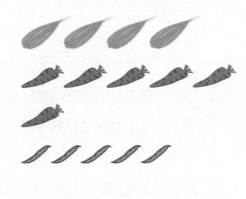

☐ 🥒 + ☐ 🥕 + ☐ 🌶 = ?

☐ + ☐ = ☐ vegetables

---

3. Casey helps gather flowers. How many flowers does Casey gather?

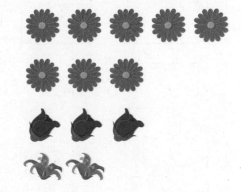

☐ 🌼 + ☐ 🌷 + ☐ 🌸 = ?

☐ + ☐ = ☐ flowers

Use the picture.
Write the numbers to solve.

4. Some carrots are in a garden.
   Each bunny eats 1 carrot.
   Now there are 9 carrots.
   How many carrots were
   in the garden to start?

[   ] – [   ] = [   ]

[   ] carrots

5. Some bunnies are in a garden.
   7 more bunnies hop in. Now there
   are 13 bunnies in the garden.
   How many bunnies were
   in the garden before?

[   ] + [   ] = [   ]

[   ] bunnies

Focus on Mathematical Practices

Find the unknown partner.

1. 8 + ☐ = 14

2. 9 + ☐ = 16

3. 6 + ☐ = 15

Subtract.

4. 13 − 9 = ☐

5. 17 − 8 = ☐

6. 15 − 7 = ☐

Solve the story problem.

Show your work. Use drawings, numbers, or words.

7. 12 frogs are on a log. Some frogs hop away. Now there are 7 frogs. How many frogs hop away?

frog

☐ _____
label

8. 18 bicycles are at the school. 9 are red and the rest are blue. How many bicycles are blue?

school

☐ _____
label

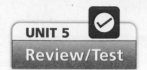
Name _____

Solve the story problem.

Show your work. Use drawings, numbers, or words.

9. There are 7 ducks on the pond. Some more ducks swim over. Now there are 13 ducks. How many ducks swim over?

pond

☐ _____
label

10. Sergio has 14 toy cars. He gives 5 of them to his brother. How many toy cars does Sergio have now?

toy car

☐ _____
label

11. I have 8 red apples, 5 green apples, and 2 yellow apples. How many apples do I have?

apple

☐ _____
label

12. Beatrix sees 9 oak trees, 4 maple trees, and 6 pine trees. How many trees does she see?

tree

☐ _____
label

© Houghton Mifflin Harcourt Publishing Company

Show your work. Use drawings, numbers, or words.

Solve the story problem.

13. There are 11 books in a box. Some are old and some are new. How many old and new books can there be? Show three answers.

book

[ ] old books and [ ] new books

or [ ] old books and [ ] new books

or [ ] old books and [ ] new books

Solve.

14. 90 + [ ] = 100

15. 30 + [ ] = 100

16. 68 + 30 = [ ]

17. 60 + 12 = [ ]

18. 70 − 50 = [ ]

19. 90 − 40 = [ ]

20. 80 − 80 = [ ]

21. 40 − 0 = [ ]

22. 60 − 50 = [ ]

23. 80 − 30 = [ ]

50 + [ ] = 60

30 + [ ] = 80

24. Start at 91. Count. Write the numbers through 120.

91	92	93							
101									

25. **Extended Response** Draw 20 to 30 more stars.
Ring 10-groups. Count by tens and ones.
Write the numbers.

☆ ☆ ☆ ☆ ☆ ☆ ☆ ☆ ☆ ☆
☆ ☆ ☆ ☆ ☆ ☆ ☆ ☆ ☆ ☆
☆ ☆ ☆ ☆ ☆ ☆ ☆ ☆ ☆ ☆
☆ ☆ ☆ ☆ ☆ ☆ ☆ ☆ ☆
☆ ☆ ☆ ☆ ☆ ☆ ☆ ☆ ☆ ☆
☆ ☆

The number of stars is [   ].

10 less is [   ]. 10 more is [   ].

Dear Family:

Children begin this unit by learning to organize, represent, and interpret data with two and three categories.

In the example below, children sort apples and bananas and represent the data using circles. They ask and answer questions about the data and learn to express comparative statements completely.

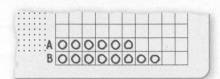

There are 2 more bananas than apples.

There are 2 fewer apples than bananas.

Later in the unit, children solve *Compare* story problems using comparison bars. Two examples are given below.

Jeremy has 10 crayons.
Amanda has 3 crayons.
How many more crayons does Jeremy have than Amanda?

J	10

A	3	?

Abby has 8 erasers.
Ramon has 6 more erasers than Abby has. How many erasers does Ramon have?

R	?

A	8	6

While working on homework, ask your child to explain to you how to use comparison bars to solve these types of story problems.

If you have any questions, please do not hesitate to contact me.

Sincerely,
Your child's teacher

COMMON CORE

This unit includes the Common Core Standards for Mathematical Content for Operations and Algebraic Thinking 1.OA.1, 1.OA.2; Measurement and Data 1.MD.4 and all Mathematical Practices.

Estimada familia:

Al comenzar esta unidad, los niños aprenderán a organizar, representar e interpretar datos de dos y tres categorías.

En el ejemplo de abajo, los niños clasifican manzanas y plátanos, y representan los datos usando círculos. Formulan y responden preguntas acerca de los datos y aprenden cómo expresar enunciados comparativos completos.

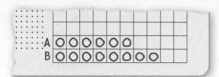

Hay 2 plátanos más que manzanas

Hay 2 manzanas menos que plátanos

Más adelante en la unidad, los niños resolverán problemas que requieran *comparar*, usando barras de comparación. Abajo se dan dos ejemplos.

Jeremy tiene 10 crayones.
Amanda tiene 3 crayones.
¿Cuántos crayones más que
Amanda tiene Jeremy?

J | 10

A | 3 | ?

Abby tiene 8 borradores.
Ramón tiene 6 borradores
más que Abby. ¿Cuántos
borradores tiene Ramón?

R | ?

A | 8 | 6

Mientras hace la tarea, pida a su niño que le explique cómo usar las barras de comparación para resolver este tipo de problemas.

Si tiene alguna pregunta, no dude en comunicarse conmigo.

Atentamente,
El maestro de su niño

COMMON CORE

Esta unidad incluye los Common Core Standards for Mathematical Content for Operations and Algebraic Thinking 1.OA.1, 1.OA.2; Measurement and Data 1.MD.4 and all Mathematical Practices.

Explore Representing Data

VOCABULARY
sort

Cut out the cards.

Which bugs have legs?

Which bugs do not have legs?

Sort the bugs.

Explore Representing Data

6-1
Class Activity

Name ______________________________

VOCABULARY
data
more
fewer

1. Use circles and 5-groups to record.
Write how many in each group.

Legs	No Legs
☐	☐

Use the **data** to complete.

2. How many bugs in all? ____________

3. Ring the group with **more** bugs.

4. Cross out the group with **fewer** bugs.

VOCABULARY
most
fewest

5. Use circles and 5-groups to record.
   Write how many in each group.

Brown	Red	Black

Use the data to complete.

6. How many bugs in all? _____

7. Ring the group with the **most** bugs.

8. Cross out the group with the **fewest** bugs.

Explore Representing Data

VOCABULARY
compare

1. Draw matching lines to **compare**.
Complete the sentences.
Ring the word **more** or **fewer**.

Mara

Todd

Mara has ☐ **more fewer** apples than Todd.

Todd has ☐ **more fewer** apples than Mara.

---

2. Each ant gets 1 crumb.
How many more crumbs are needed? ☐

3. Draw circles
for the crumbs.

Crumbs	🔘 🔘 🔘 🔘
Ants	🐜 🐜 🐜 🐜 🐜 🐜 🐜 🐜 🐜 🐜

---

4. Each bee gets 1 flower. How many extra flowers are there? ☐

5. Ring the
extra flowers.

Flowers	🌹 🌹 🌹 🌹 🌹 🌹 🌹 🌹 🌹
Bees	🐝 🐝 🐝 🐝

6. Sort the fruit. Record with pictures.
Write how many in each group.

Bananas											_____
Oranges											_____

7. Complete the sentences. Ring the word **more** or **fewer**.

There are [ ] **more fewer** bananas than oranges.

There are [ ] **more fewer** oranges than bananas.

---

8. Sort the vegetables. Record with circles.
Write how many in each group.

Carrots											_____
Peppers											_____

9. Complete the sentences. Ring the word **more** or **fewer**.

There are [ ] **more fewer** peppers than carrots.

There are [ ] **more fewer** carrots than peppers.

Organize Categorical Data

1. Look at what Puzzled Penguin wrote.

Am I correct?

Stripes	O	O	O	O	O	O	O	O	O
Spots	O	O	O	O	O				

There are 4 more fish with stripes than with spots.

There are 4 fewer fish with spots than with stripes.

2. Help Puzzled Penguin.

Stripes									
Spots									

There are ☐ more fish with stripes than with spots.

There are ☐ fewer fish with spots than with stripes.

3. Sort the animals. Record with circles.
   Write how many in each group.

Dogs									____
Cats									____

4. Complete the sentences. Ring the word **more** or **fewer**.

There are ☐ **more fewer** cats than dogs.

There are ☐ **more fewer** dogs than cats.

(PATH to FLUENCY) Add.

1.	4	2.	8	3.	5	4.	10	5.	4
	+3		+1		+5		+0		+6

Use Stair Steps to Represent Data

1. Discuss the data.

2. Write how many in each category.

Eggs Laid This Month

Clucker	🥚🥚🥚🥚	_____
Vanilla	🥚🥚🥚🥚🥚🥚🥚🥚🥚	_____
Daisy	🥚🥚🥚🥚🥚🥚🥚	_____

Animals in the Pond

Frogs	🐸🐸🐸🐸🐸🐸	_____
Fish	🐟🐟🐟🐟🐟🐟🐟	_____
Ducks	🦆🦆🦆🦆	_____

Hot Dogs Sold at the Fair

Eric	🌭🌭🌭🌭🌭🌭🌭🌭	_____
Miranda	🌭🌭🌭🌭🌭🌭	_____
Adam	🌭🌭🌭🌭🌭	_____

Watch as each cube is taken from the bag.

3. Draw circles to show how many of each color.

Colors in the Bag									
Red									
Yellow									
Blue									

Use the data to answer the questions.

4. How many red cubes are in the bag? _____

5. How many yellow cubes are in the bag? _____

6. How many blue cubes are in the bag? _____

7. How many more blue cubes are there than red cubes?

   _____

8. How many fewer red cubes are there than yellow cubes?

   _____

9. There are the most of which color? _____

10. There are the fewest of which color? _____

11. How many cubes are there in all? _____

Data Sets with Three Categories

VOCABULARY
comparison bars

Solve the story problem.
Use **comparison bars**.

Show your work.

1. Tessa has 15 pens.
   Sam has 9 pens.
   How many more pens
   does Tessa have than Sam?

   ☐ _____
       label

2. Tessa has 15 pens.
   Sam has 9 pens.
   How many fewer pens
   does Sam have than Tessa?

   ☐ _____
       label

3. Tessa has 15 pens.
   Sam has 6 fewer pens than Tessa.
   How many pens does Sam have?

   ☐ _____
       label

4. Sam has 9 pens.
   Tessa has 6 more than Sam.
   How many pens does Tessa have?

   ☐ _____
       label

Solve the story problem.   **Show your work.**
Use comparison bars.

5. Dan reads 9 books.
   Ana reads 11 books.
   How many fewer books
   does Dan read than Ana?

   [ ] _____
        label

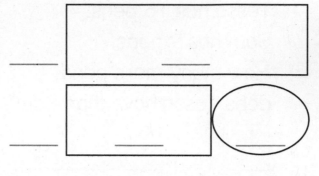

6. Luis makes 7 eggs for breakfast.
   Emily makes 3 eggs.
   How many more eggs
   does Luis make than Emily?

   [ ] _____
        label

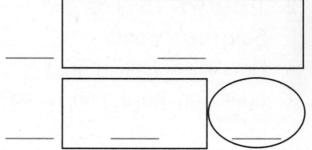

7. Noah has 10 more caps than Ben.
   Ben has 10 caps.
   How many caps does Noah have?

   [ ] _____
        label

8. Jen eats 2 fewer carrots than Scott.
   Scott eats 9 carrots.
   How many carrots does Jen eat?

   [ ] _____
        label

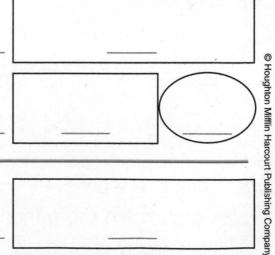

Solve and discuss.

1. There are 14 tigers and 8 bears. How many more tigers than bears are there?

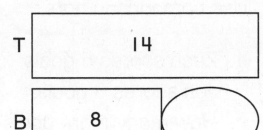

T | 14

B | 8

☐ _____
         label

$14 = 8 +$ ☐

$14 - 8 =$ ☐

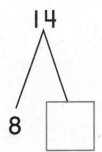

14

8

___

2. There are 12 lions. There are 5 fewer camels than lions. How many camels are there?

L | 12

C | ☐ | 5

☐ _____
         label

$5 +$ ☐ $= 12$

$12 - 5 =$ ☐

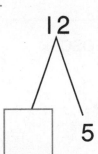

12

5

3. There are 7 elephants. There are 6 more zebras than elephants. How many zebras are there?

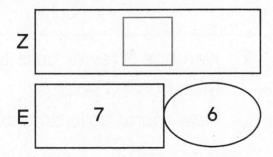

Z | ☐

E | 7 | 6

☐ _____
         label

$7 + 6 =$ ☐

Solve the story problem.
Use comparison bars.

Show your work.

---

4. Zach scores 5 goals.

   Jon scores 8 goals.

   How many more goals

   does Jon score than Zach?

   ☐ _____
   label

---

5. There are 11 cars and 19

   trucks on the road. How many

   fewer cars are there than trucks?

   ☐ _____
   label

---

6. I see 8 more lilacs than roses.

   I see 9 roses.

   How many lilacs do I see?

   ☐ _____
   label

---

7. Ken has 3 fewer balls than Meg.

   Meg has 10 balls.

   How many balls does Ken have?

   ☐ _____
   label

Comparison Bars and Comparing Language

Solve the story problem.   **Show your work.**
Use comparison bars.

1. Cory's cat has 11 kittens.
   Eva's cat has 3 kittens.
   How many fewer kittens does
   Eva's cat have than Cory's?

   ☐ _____
              label

2. There were 3 bicycles here
   yesterday. There are 7 more
   bicycles here today. How many
   bicycles are here today?

   ☐ _____
              label

3. Ms. Perez has 15 horses.
   Mr. Drew has 9 horses.
   How many more horses does
   Ms. Perez have than Mr. Drew?

   ☐ _____
              label

Name _____

Solve the story problem.
Use comparison bars.

Show your work.

---

4. Jim pops 5 fewer balloons than
Sadie. Jim pops 9 balloons. How
many balloons does Sadie pop?

☐ _____
label

---

5. Nick hikes 12 miles in the forest.
Nick hikes 4 more miles than Zia.
How many miles does Zia hike?

☐ _____
label

PATH to FLUENCY Subtract.

1.	2.	3.	4.	5.
9 − 1	6 − 3	8 − 6	5 − 5	9 − 7

6.	7.	8.	9.	10.
4 − 2	10 − 6	9 − 3	7 − 5	6 − 1

11.	12.	13.	14.	15.
8 − 7	9 − 4	7 − 7	10 − 5	8 − 1

Solve Compare Problems

► **Math and the Park**

Liam collects data at the park. He wants to know how many animals can fly and how many animals cannot fly.

1. Sort the animals.

   Record with circles and 5-groups.

Animals That Can Fly	Animals That Cannot Fly

Use the data to complete.

2. How many animals can fly? _____

3. How many animals cannot fly? _____

4. How many animals does Liam see in all? _____

5. How many more animals can fly than cannot fly?

   _____

Solve.

Show your work.

6. There are 8 swings.
12 children want to swing.
How many children must
wait to swing?

☐ _____

---

7. 10 bikes are on the rack.
7 children start to ride.
How many bikes do not
have a rider?

☐ _____

1. Sort the bugs. Record with circles.

2. Write how many in each group.

Stripes									
Spots									
Solid									

Use the data to complete.

3. How many more bugs with stripes are
   there than bugs with spots? _____

4. How many fewer solid color bugs are there
   than bugs with stripes? _____

5. How many bugs are there in all? _____

Solve the story problem.   **Show your work.**
Use comparison bars.

---

6. Nina has 9 stamps.
   Jan has 14 stamps.
   How many more stamps
   does Jan have than Nina?

   ☐ _____
          label

---

7. I see 6 fewer turtles than frogs.
   I see 13 frogs.
   How many turtles do I see?

   ☐ _____
          label

---

8. Dasha eats 8 grapes.
   Alex eats 17 grapes.
   How many fewer grapes
   does Dasha eat than Alex?

   ☐ _____
          label

---

9. Ed knits 4 more hats than scarves.
   Ed knits 8 scarves.
   How many hats does Ed knit?

   ☐ _____
          label

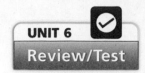
10. Extended Response A class wants to choose a pet. They collect data about favorite pets. Each child votes. The teacher draws one circle for each vote.

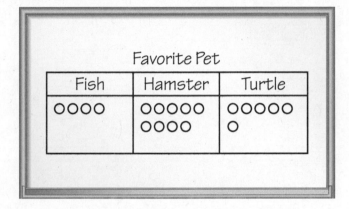

Favorite Pet

Fish	Hamster	Turtle
OOOO	OOOOO OOOO	OOOOO O

Write and answer two questions about the data.

_____

- -

_____

- -

_____

- -

_____

- -

_____

- -

Family Letter

Dear Family:

Your child has begun a unit that focuses on measurement and geometry. Children will begin the unit by learning to tell and write time in hours and half-hours on an analog and digital clock.

2:00

hour : minute

Later in the unit, children will work with both 2-dimensional and 3-dimensional shapes.

They will learn to distinguish between defining and non-defining attributes of shapes. For example, rectangles have four sides and four square corners. A square is a special kind of rectangle with all sides the same length. The shapes below are different sizes, colors, and orientations, but they are all rectangles.

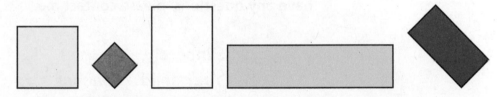

Later in the unit, children will compose shapes to create new shapes.

 A cone and a rectangular prism were used to make this new shape.

Children will also learn to partition circles and rectangles into two and four equal shares. They describe the shares using the words *halves*, *fourths*, and *quarters*.

 This circle is partitioned into halves.

 This circle is partitioned into fourths or quarters.

Children generalize that partitioning a shape into more equal shares creates smaller shares: one fourth of the circle above is smaller than one half of the circle.

Another concept in this unit is length measurement. Children order three objects by length.

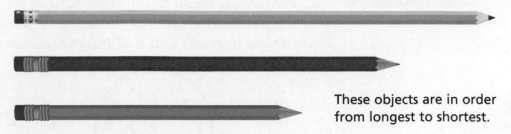

These objects are in order from longest to shortest.

They also use same-size length units such as paper clips to measure the length of an object.

This ribbon is 4 paper clips long.

You can help your child practice these new skills at home. If you have any questions, please contact me.

Sincerely,
Your child's teacher

COMMON CORE This unit includes the Common Core Standards for Mathematical Content for Measurement and Data 1.MD.1, 1.MD.2, 1.MD.3; Geometry 1.G.1, 1.G.2, 1.G.3 and all Mathematical Practices.

Carta a la familia

Estimada familia:

Su niño ha comenzado una unidad sobre medidas y geometría. Comenzará esta unidad aprendiendo a leer y escribir la hora en punto y la media hora en un reloj analógico y en uno digital.

2:00

hora : minuto

Después, trabajará con figuras bidimensionales y tridimensionales.

Aprenderá a distinguir entre atributos que definen a una figura y los que no la definen. Por ejemplo, los rectángulos tienen cuatro lados y cuatro esquinas. Un cuadrado es un tipo especial de rectángulo que tiene lados de igual longitud. Las figuras de abajo tienen diferente tamaño, color y orientación, pero todas son rectángulos.

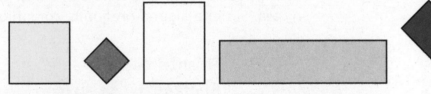

Más adelante en la unidad, los niños acomodarán figuras de diferentes maneras para formar nuevas figuras.

 Para formar esta nueva figura se usaron un cono y un prisma rectangular.

También aprenderán a dividir círculos y rectángulos en dos y cuatro partes iguales. Describirán esas partes usando *mitades* y *cuartos*.

 Este círculo está dividido en mitades.

 Este círculo está dividido en cuartos.

Deducirán que si dividen un figura en más partes iguales, obtendrán partes más pequeñas: un cuarto del círculo es más pequeño que una mitad.

Otro concepto que se enseña en esta unidad es la medición de longitudes. Los niños ordenan tres objetos según su longitud.

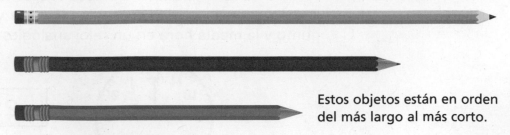

Estos objetos están en orden del más largo al más corto.

También usan unidades de la misma longitud, tales como clips, para medir la longitud de un objeto.

Esta cinta mide 4 clips de longitud.

Usted puede ayudar a su niño a practicar estas nuevas destrezas en casa. Si tiene alguna pregunta, comuníquese conmigo.

Atentamente,
El maestro de su niño

COMMON CORE   Esta unidad incluye los Common Core Standards for Mathematical Content for Measurement and Data 1.MD.1, 1.MD.2, 1.MD.3; Geometry 1.G.1, 1.G.2, 1.G.3 and all Mathematical Practices.

Student Clock (with hands) **199**

Read the **clock**.
Write the time on the digital clock.

1.

2:00
hour : minute

2.

:
hour : minute

3.

:

4.

:

5.

:

6.

:

7.

:

8.

:

9.

:

10.

:

Draw the **hour hand** on the clock
to show the time.

11.

4:00

12.

10:00

13.

5:00

14.

8:00

15. Look at the hour hand Puzzled Penguin drew.

3:00

Am I correct?

16. Help Puzzled Penguin.

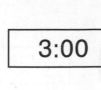
3:00

Tell and Write Time in Hours

Name

Clocks for "Our Busy Day" Book

Clocks for "Our Busy Day" Book **203**

Read the clock.
Write the time on the digital clock.

1.

```
  :
```
hour : minute

2.

```
  :
```
hour : minute

3.

```
  :
```

4.

```
  :
```

Draw the hour hand on the clock
to show the time.

5.

```
6:00
```

6.

```
9:00
```

7.

```
8:00
```

8.

```
7:00
```

9.

```
4:00
```

10.

```
3:00
```

Name _____

Fill in the numbers on the clock.

Choose an hour time.

Draw the hands to show the time. Write the time.

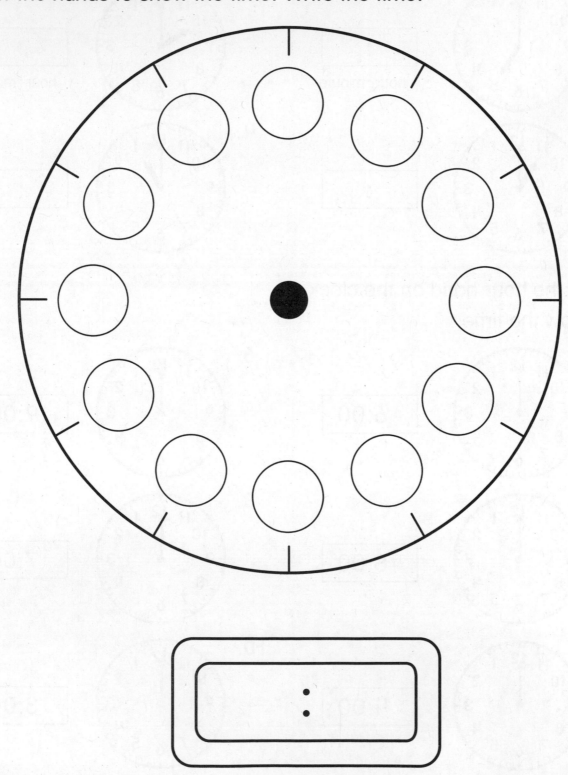

Class Activity

Name _____

Read the clock.

Write the **half-hour** time on the digital clock.

1.

☐ : ☐

hour : minute

2.

☐ : ☐

hour : minute

3.

☐ : ☐

4.

☐ : ☐

5.

☐ : ☐

6.

☐ : ☐

7.

☐ : ☐

8.

☐ : ☐

9.

☐ : ☐

10.

☐ : ☐

Tell and Write Time in Half-Hours

Ring the clock that shows the correct time.
Cross out the clock that shows the wrong time.

11.

7:30

12.

4:30

13.

12:30

14.

9:30

15. Look at the hour hand Puzzled Penguin drew.

1:30

Am I correct?

16. Help Puzzled Penguin.

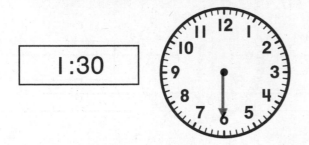

1:30

Show the same half-hour time on both clocks.

1.

[clock face]

:

2.

[clock face]

:

3.

[clock face]

:

4.

[clock face]

:

5.

[clock face]

:

6.

[clock face]

:

7.

[clock face]

:

8.

[clock face]

:

9.

[clock face]

:

Name _____

Show the same time on both clocks.
Pick hour and half-hour times.

10.	11.	12.
:	:	:

13.	14.	15.
:	:	:

PATH to FLUENCY **Add.**

1. $7 + 2 = \square$ 2. $5 + 3 = \square$ 3. $7 + 1 = \square$

4. $5 + 5 = \square$ 5. $8 + 2 = \square$ 6. $6 + 3 = \square$

PATH to FLUENCY **Find the unknown partner.**

7. $4 + \square = 8$ 8. $4 + \square = 10$ 9. $8 + \square = 9$

Practice Telling and Writing Time

2-Dimensional Shape Set

2-Dimensional Shape Set

1. Which shapes are NOT **rectangles** or **squares**?
   Draw an X on each one.

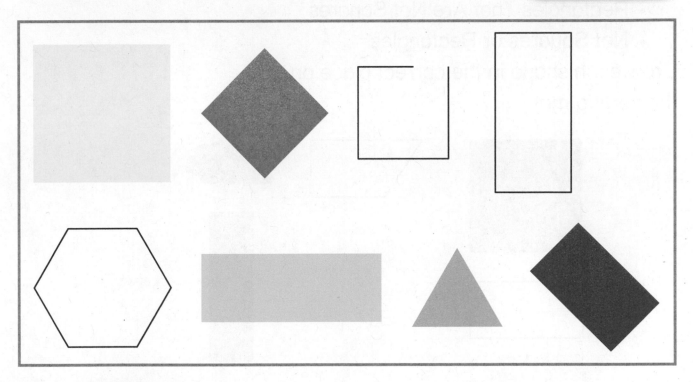

Draw the shape.

2. 4 **sides**,
   4 **square corners**

3. 4 sides the same length,
   4 square corners

4. Sort the shapes into three groups:
   - Squares
   - Rectangles That Are Not Squares
   - Not Squares or Rectangles

Draw each shape in the correct place on the sorting mat.

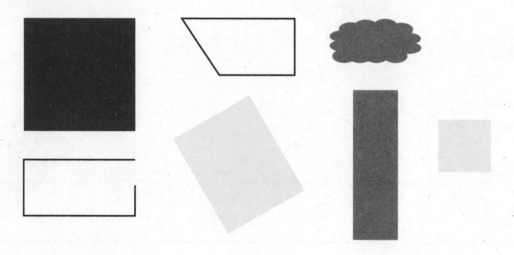

Squares	Rectangles That Are Not Squares	Not Squares or Rectangles

VOCABULARY
triangles
circles

I. Which shapes are NOT **triangles** or **circles**?
Draw an X on each one.

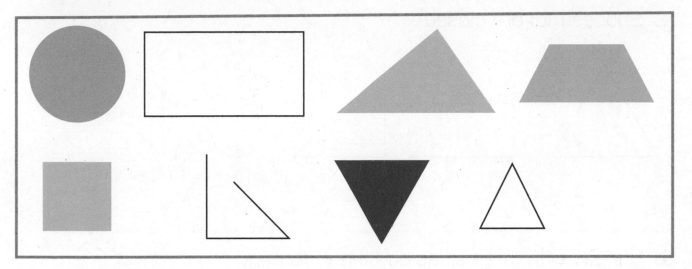

Draw the shape.

2. closed, 3 sides, 3 corners	3. closed, no corners

Name

Ring the shapes that follow the sorting rule.
Draw a shape that fits the rule.

4. Shapes that are closed

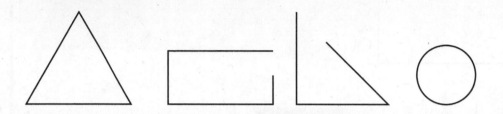

5. Shapes with three sides and three corners

6. Shapes with a square corner

VOCABULARY
halves

Cut out the shapes below.
How many ways can you fold them into **halves**?

Draw a line to show halves.
Color one **half of** the shape.

1.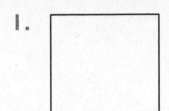

2.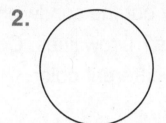

3.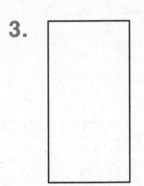

4.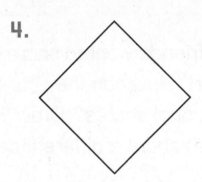

Draw lines to show **fourths**.
Color one **fourth of** the shape.

5.

6.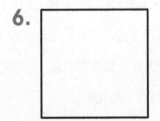

7.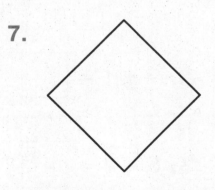

8.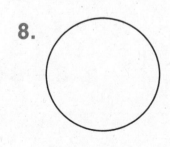

Name

Solve the story problem.

9. Four friends want to share a sandwich.
How can they cut the sandwich into four
equal shares? Draw lines. Color
each share a different color.

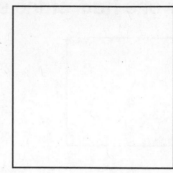

10. The four friends want to share a pie
for dessert. How can they cut the pie
into four equal shares? Draw lines.
Color each share a different color.

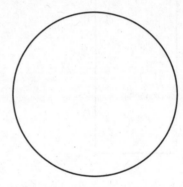

11. One friend only wants one half of her
granola bar. How can she cut her
granola bar into halves? Draw a line
to show two equal shares. Color each
share a different color.

PATH to FLUENCY Subtract.

1. $10 - 3 =$ ☐   2. $8 - 8 =$ ☐   3. $9 - 1 =$ ☐

4. $6 - 5 =$ ☐   5. $7 - 5 =$ ☐   6. $5 - 4 =$ ☐

Equal Shares

Build and draw the shape.

1. Build a square. Use rectangles.

_____

2. Build a rectangle with all sides the same length.
   Use triangles with a square corner.

_____

3. Build a rectangle with two short sides and two
   long sides. Use triangles and rectangles.

Compose 2-Dimensional Shapes

Use ▊ to make the new shape.

7. Use ▦ to make
the new shape.

4.

5.

6.

Compose 2-Dimensional Shapes

Draw a line to match like shapes.
Write the name of the shape.

1.  _____

2.   _____

3. 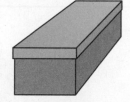 _____

4.   _____

5.  _____

VOCABULARY
rectangular prisms
cubes

6. Which shapes are NOT **rectangular prisms**?
Draw an X on each one.

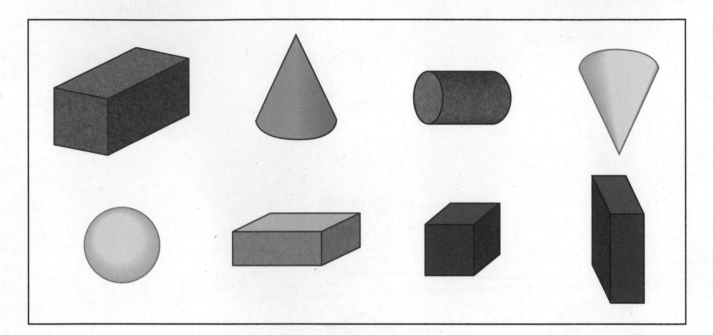

7. Ring the shapes that are **cubes**.

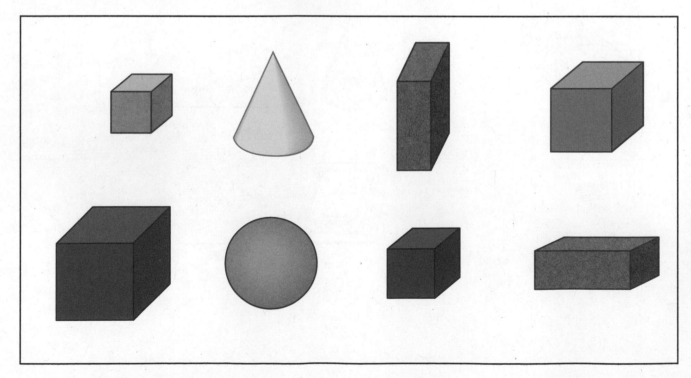

Ring the shapes used to make the new shape.

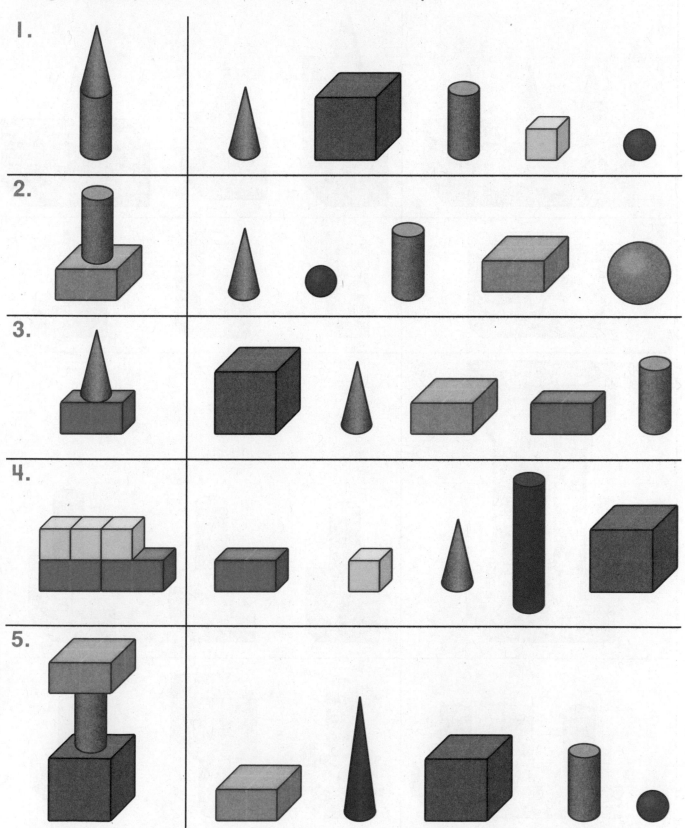

1.

2.

3.

4.

5.

Compose 3-Dimensional Shapes **229**

Name _____

Ring the shape used to make the larger shape.

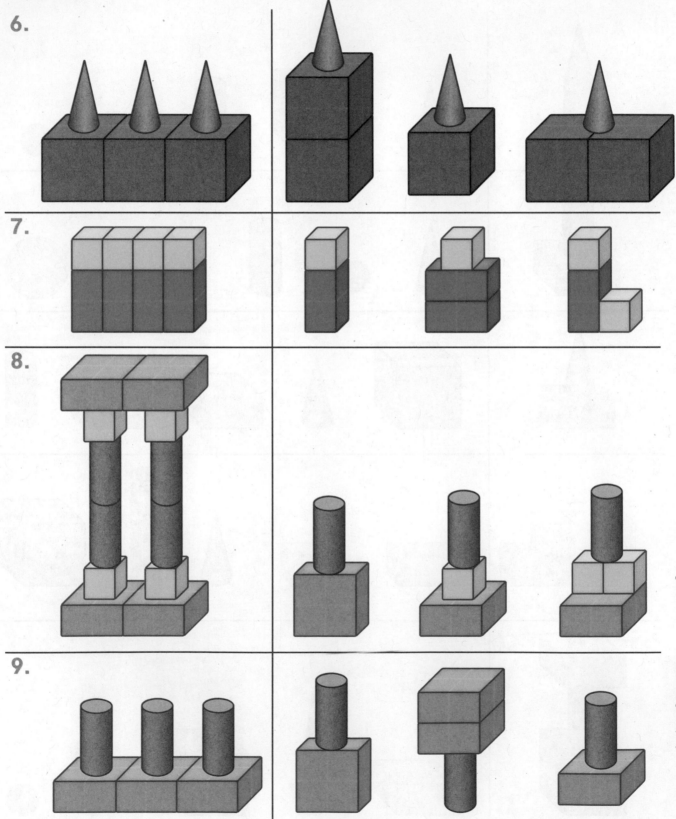

6.

7.

8.

9.

Compose 3-Dimensional Shapes

Write 1, 2, 3 to order from shortest to longest.

1.

☐

☐

☐

2.

☐

☐

☐

© Houghton Mifflin Harcourt Publishing Company

Draw three different lines.

Write 1, 2, 3 to order from longest to shortest.

3.

4.

Order by Length

Name _____

Measure in paper clips.

1. Red ribbon   How long? ☐ paper clips

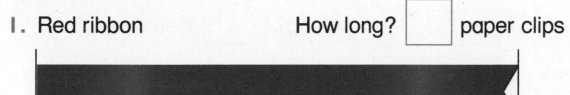

2. Blue ribbon   How long? ☐ paper clips

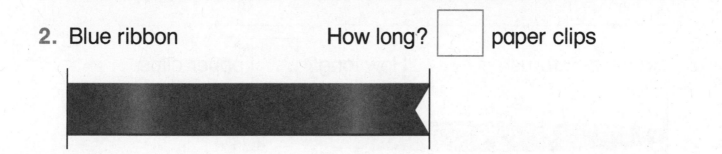

3. Green pencil   How long? ☐ paper clips

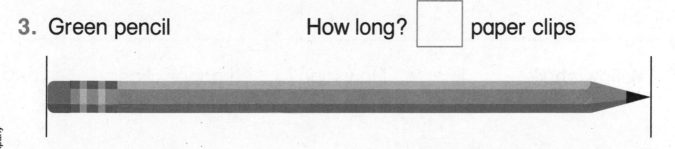

4. Purple pencil   How long? ☐ paper clips

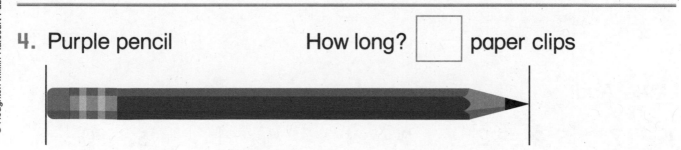

Measure in paper clips.

5. Orange crayon   How long? ☐ paper clips

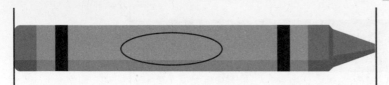

6. Brown paintbrush   How long? ☐ paper clips

7. Yellow chalk   How long? ☐ paper clips

PATH to FLUENCY Add.

1.	7	2.	2	3.	4	4.	1	5.	0
	+3		+6		+5		+7		+9

Measure with Length Units

▶ Math and a Picnic

Jay and his family are going on a picnic.
Draw lines to show equal shares.

1. Jay wants to share his burger
   with his mom. How can he cut
   his burger into two equal shares?

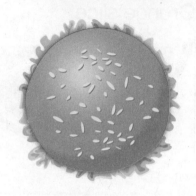

2. Jay and his three sisters want
   to share a pan of corn bread.
   How can he cut the bread into
   four equal shares?

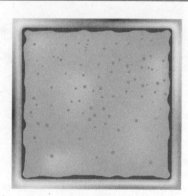

3. Jay's mom and his three
   sisters want to share a block of
   cheese. How can they cut the
   block of cheese into four
   equal shares?

© Houghton Mifflin Harcourt Publishing Company • Image Credits: ©Fancy/Alamy Images

There will be lots of food at the picnic.
Measure the food in small paper clips.

4. Orange slice

How long? ☐ paper clips

---

5. Celery

How long? ☐ paper clips

---

6. Cracker

How long? ☐ paper clips

---

7. Order the picnic food from longest
to shortest. Write the names.

Read the clock.

Write the time on the digital clock.

1.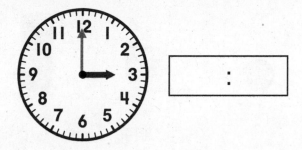

2.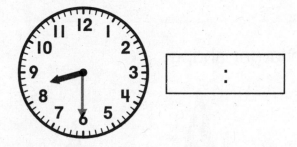

3. Which shapes are NOT triangles?

Draw an X on each one.

4. Ring the shapes used to make the new shape.

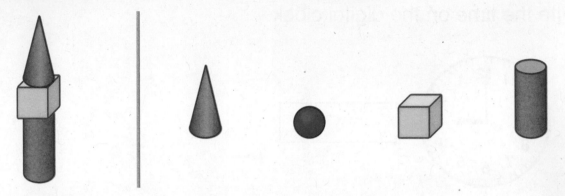

5. Ring the shape used to make the larger shape.

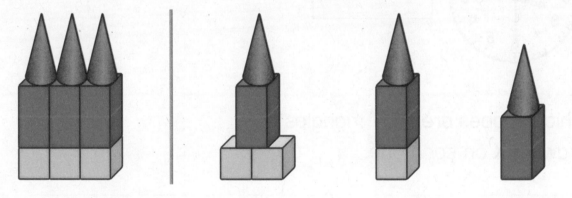

6. Draw a line to show halves.
Color one half of the shape.

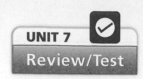
7. Draw lines to show fourths.
Color one fourth of the shape.

---

8. Write 1, 2, 3 in order from longest to shortest.

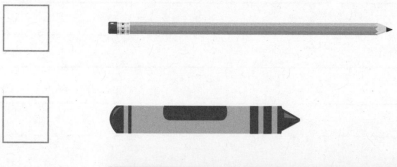

---

9. Measure in paper clips.

How long? ☐ paper clips

10. Extended Response Eli has this crayon and this pencil.

Sam gives him an eraser that is shorter than the crayon.

Is the eraser shorter than the pencil? Explain.

_____

- -

_____

- -

_____

- -

_____

- -

_____

- -

_____

- -

Family Letter

Dear Family:

Your child will be using special drawings of 10-sticks and circles to add greater numbers. The sticks show the number of tens, and the circles show the number of ones. When a new group of ten is made, a ring is drawn around it.

There are several ways for children to show the new group of ten when they add 2-digit numbers.

- Children can do the addition with a single total. The 1 for the new ten can be written either below the tens column or above it. Writing it below makes addition easier because the 1 new ten is added after children have added the two numbers that are already there. Also, children can see the 16 they made from 7 and 9 because the 1 and 6 are closer together than they were when the new ten was written above.

$$\begin{array}{r} 27 \\ + 49 \\ \hline 76 \end{array}$$ new ten below

$$\begin{array}{r} {}^{1}\ \\ 27 \\ + 49 \\ \hline 76 \end{array}$$ new ten above

- Children can make separate totals for tens and ones. Many first-graders prefer to work from left to right because that is how they read. They add the tens (20 + 40 = 60) and then the ones (7 + 9 = 16). The last step is to add the two totals together (60 + 16 = 76).

$$\begin{array}{r} 27 \\ + 49 \\ \hline 60 \\ 16 \\ \hline 76 \end{array}$$ left to right

$$\begin{array}{r} 27 \\ + 49 \\ \hline 16 \\ 60 \\ \hline 76 \end{array}$$ right to left

You may notice your child using one of these methods as he or she completes homework.

Sincerely,
Your child's teacher

COMMON CORE Unit 8 includes the Common Core Standards for Mathematical Content for Number and Operations in Base Ten 1.NBT.4 and all Mathematical Practices.

Carta a la familia

Estimada familia:

Su niño usará dibujos especiales de palitos de decenas y círculos para sumar números más grandes. Los palitos muestran el número de decenas y los círculos muestran el número de unidades. Cuando se forma un nuevo grupo de diez, se encierra.

Hay varias maneras en las que los niños pueden mostrar el nuevo grupo de diez al sumar números de 2 dígitos.

• Pueden hacer la suma con un total único. El 1 que indica la nueva decena se puede escribir abajo o arriba de la columna de las decenas. Escribirlo abajo hace que la suma sea más fácil porque la nueva decena se suma después de sumar los dos números que ya estaban allí. Además, los niños pueden ver el 16 que obtuvieron de 7 y 9 porque el 1 y el 6 están más juntos que cuando la nueva decena estaba escrita arriba.

$$\begin{array}{r} 27 \\ +\,49 \\ \hline {}_1 \\ 76 \end{array}$$ nueva decena abajo

$$\begin{array}{r} {}^1 \\ 27 \\ +\,49 \\ \hline 76 \end{array}$$ nueva decena arriba

• Pueden hacer totales separados para decenas y para unidades. Muchos estudiantes de primer grado prefieren trabajar de izquierda a derecha porque así leen. Suman las decenas (20 + 40 = 60) y luego las unidades (7 + 9 = 16). El último paso es sumar ambos totales (60 + 16 = 76).

$$\begin{array}{r} 27 \\ +\,49 \\ \hline 60 \\ 16 \\ \hline 76 \end{array}$$ de izquierda a derecha

$$\begin{array}{r} 27 \\ +\,49 \\ \hline 16 \\ 60 \\ \hline 76 \end{array}$$ de derecha a izquierda

Es posible que su niño use uno de estos métodos al hacer la tarea.

Atentamente,
El maestro de su niño

COMMON CORE La Unidad 8 incluye los Common Core Standards for Mathematical Content for Number and Operations in Base Ten 1.NBT.4 and all Mathematical Practices.

Explore 2-Digit Addition

Uncle David
28 Apples

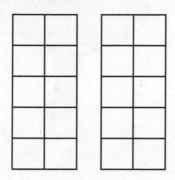

28
apples

16
apples

Put extra apples here.

Aunt Sarah
16 Apples

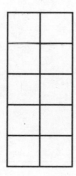

Put extra apples here.

Total Apples

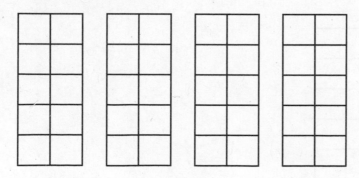

Put extra apples here.

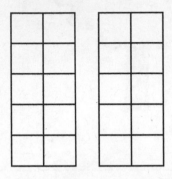

Name _____

Uncle David
26 Apples

26 apples

20 apples

Put extra apples here.

Aunt Sarah
20 Apples

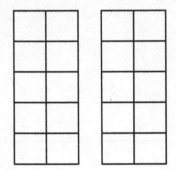

Put extra apples here.

Total Apples

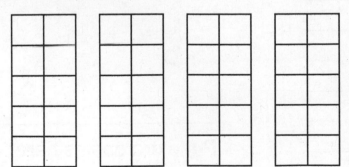

Put extra apples here.

Explore 2-Digit Addition

47 apples

19 apples

26 apples

13 apples

25 apples

34 apples

51 apples

29 apples

37 apples

48 apples

1. Work in pairs. Each child chooses one apple tree.

2. On your MathBoard or paper, add the apples in the two trees.

3. Check to see if you both got the same answer.

4. Repeat with other trees.

5. Work in pairs. One child chooses one apple tree with a 2-digit number. The other child chooses another tree.

6. On your MathBoard or paper, add the apples in the two trees.

7. Check to see if you both got the same answer.

8. Repeat with other trees.

1. Work in pairs. Each child chooses one peach tree.

2. On your MathBoard or paper, add the peaches in the two trees.

3. Check to see if you both got the same answer.

4. Repeat with other trees.

5. **Discuss** For which problems did you make a new ten?

Add.

6.   53
      + 38

7.   16
      + 6

8.   67
      + 15

9.   72
      + 20

10.   56
      + 13

11.   47
      + 30

12.   48
      + 5

13.   82
      + 14

14.   17
      + 2

Write the vertical form. Then add.

15. 65 + 8

16. 6 + 73

17. 56 + 28

18. 38 + 40

Add.

1. 93
   + 6

2. 28
   + 18

3. 66
   + 7

4. 49
   + 30

5. 56
   + 25

6. 15
   + 4

Write the vertical form. Then add.

7. 71 + 19

8. 54 + 20

9. 33 + 29

10. 44 + 4

11. 8 + 74

12. 19 + 67

13. Look at the total Puzzled Penguin wrote.

$$\begin{array}{r} 43 \\ + 39 \\ \hline 712 \end{array}$$

Am I correct?

14. Help Puzzled Penguin.

$$\begin{array}{r} 43 \\ + 39 \\ \hline \end{array}$$

PATH to FLUENCY Add.

1. 5 + 2 = ☐

2. 7 + 1 = ☐

3. 3 + 2 = ☐

4. ☐ = 8 + 2

5. ☐ = 3 + 6

6. ☐ = 4 + 3

7. 5 + 1 = ☐

8. 6 + 2 = ☐

9. 5 + 3 = ☐

10. ☐ = 7 + 2

11. ☐ = 4 + 2

12. ☐ = 2 + 1

Practice 2-Digit Addition

► **Math and the Grocery Store**

Use the pictures to solve.

1. How many potatoes are there?

49 potatoes   47 potatoes

 potatoes

2. How many cartons of milk are there?

37 cartons of milk   23 cartons of milk

 cartons of milk

3. 20 cartons of milk spill.
   How many cartons of milk are there now?

 cartons of milk

Use the pictures to solve.

4. How many jars of honey are there?

23 jars of honey   36 jars of honey

☐ jars of honey

5. How many jars of jam are there?

27 jars of jam   34 jars of jam

☐ jars of jam

6. Compare the number of jars of honey to the number of jars of jam. Write the comparison 2 ways.

Name _____

Add.

1. 56
  + 28

2. 42
  + 35

3. 65
  + 9

4. 28
  + 30

Write the vertical form. Then add.

5. 62 + 20

6. 51 + 37

7. 28 + 29

8. 74 + 5

9. How many peaches are there in all?
Show your work.

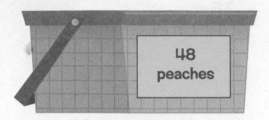

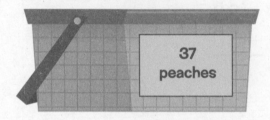

label

10. Extended Response Write an addition
exercise that you must make a new ten to
solve. Use two 2-digit numbers. Make a
Proof Drawing.

Problem Types

	Result Unknown	Change Unknown	Start Unknown
Add To	Six children are playing tag in the yard. Three more children come to play. How many children are playing in the yard now? *Situation and Solution Equation[1]:* $6 + 3 = \square$	Six children are playing tag in the yard. Some more children come to play. Now there are 9 children in the yard. How many children came to play? *Situation Equation:* $6 + \square = 9$ *Solution Equation:* $9 - 6 = \square$	Some children are playing tag in the yard. Three more children come to play. Now there are 9 children in the yard. How many children were in the yard at first? *Situation Equation:* $\square + 3 = 9$ *Solution Equation:* $9 - 3 = \square$
Take From	Jake has 10 trading cards. He gives 3 to his brother. How many trading cards does he have left? *Situation and Solution Equation:* $10 - 3 = \square$	Jake has 10 trading cards. He gives some to his brother. Now Jake has 7 trading cards left. How many cards does he give to his brother? *Situation Equation:* $10 - \square = 7$ *Solution Equation:* $10 - 7 = \square$	Jake has some trading cards. He gives 3 to his brother. Now Jake has 7 trading cards left. How many cards does he start with? *Situation Equation:* $\square - 3 = 7$ *Solution Equation:* $7 + 3 = \square$

[1]A situation equation represents the structure (action) in the problem situation. A solution equation shows the operation used to find the answer.

Problem Types (continued)

	Total Unknown	Addend Unknown	Both Addends Unknown
Put Together/ Take Apart	There are 9 red roses and 4 yellow roses in a vase. How many roses are in the vase? *Math Drawing²:* *Situation and Solution Equation:* $9 + 4 = \square$	Thirteen roses are in the vase. 9 are red and the rest are yellow. How many roses are yellow? *Math Drawing:* *Situation Equation:* $13 = 9 + \square$ *Solution Equation:* $13 - 9 = \square$	Ana has 13 roses. How many can she put in her red vase and how many in her blue vase? *Math Drawing:* *Situation Equation:* $13 = \square + \square$

²These math drawings are called Math Mountains in Grades 1—3 and break-apart drawings in Grades 4 and 5.

	Difference Unknown	Bigger Unknown	Smaller Unknown
Compare[3]	Aki has 8 apples. Sofia has 14 apples. How many **more** apples does **Sofia** have than Aki? Aki has 8 apples. Sofia has 14 apples. How many **fewer** apples does **Aki** have than Sofia? *Math Drawing:* S ▭ 14 A ▭ 8 (?) *Situation Equation:* $8 + \square = 14$ *Solution Equation:* $14 - 8 = \square$	**Leading Language** Aki has 8 apples. **Sofia** has **6 more** apples than Aki. How many apples does Sofia have? **Misleading Language** Aki has 8 apples. **Aki** has **6 fewer** apples than Sofia. How many apples does Sofia have? *Math Drawing:* S ▭ ? A ▭ 8 (6) *Situation and Solution Equation:* $8 + 6 = \square$	**Leading Language** Sofia has 14 apples. **Aki** has **6 fewer** apples than Sofia. How many apples does Aki have? **Misleading Language** Sofia has 14 apples. **Sofia** has **6 more** apples than Aki. How many apples does Aki have? *Math Drawing:* S ▭ 14 A ▭ ? (6) *Situation Equation:* $\square + 6 = 14$ *Solution Equation:* $14 - 6 = \square$

[3]A comparison sentence can always be said in two ways. One way uses *more*, and the other uses *fewer* or *less*. Misleading language suggests the wrong operation. For example, it says *Aki has 6 fewer apples than Sofia*, but you have to add 6 to Aki's 8 apples to get 14 apples.

Glossary

5-group

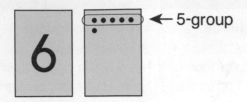

← 5-group

10-group

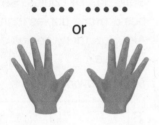

or

10-stick

||| ○○ You can show 32 with three **10-sticks** and two ones.

add

$3 + 2 = 5$

●●● ●●

addend

$5 + 4 = 9$ $5 + 4 + 8 = 17$

↑ ↑   ↑ ↑ ↑

addends   addends
(partners)

addition story problem

There are 5 ducks.
Then 3 more come.
How many ducks are there now?

---

break-apart

You can **break apart** the number 4.

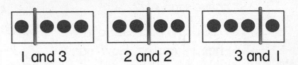

1 and 3   2 and 2   3 and 1

1 and 3, 2 and 2, and 3 and 1 are
break-aparts of 4.

circle

circle drawing

$3 + 4$ $9 - 5$

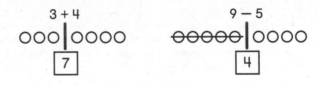

7   4

clock

analog clock

digital clock

column

1	11	21	31	41	51	61	71	81	91
2	12	22	32	42	52	62	72	82	92
3	13	23	33	43	53	63	73	83	93
4	14	24	34	44	54	64	74	84	94
5	15	25	35	45	55	65	75	85	95
6	16	26	36	46	56	66	76	86	96
7	17	27	37	47	57	67	77	87	97
8	18	28	38	48	58	68	78	88	98
9	19	29	39	49	59	69	79	89	99
10	20	30	40	50	60	70	80	90	100

compare

You can **compare** numbers.

11 is less than 12.

$$11 < 12$$

12 is greater than 11.

$$12 > 11$$

You can **compare** objects by length.

The crayon is shorter than the pencil.

The pencil is longer than the crayon.

comparison bars

Joe has 6 roses. Sasha has 9 roses. How many more roses does Sasha have than Joe?

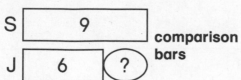

comparison bars

cone

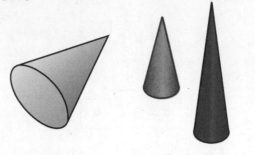

corner

corner

count

count all

$$5 + 4 = \boxed{9}$$

1 2 3 4 5   6 7 8 9

Glossary (continued)

count on

$5 + 4 = \boxed{9}$

$5 + \boxed{4} = 9$

$9 - 5 = \boxed{4}$

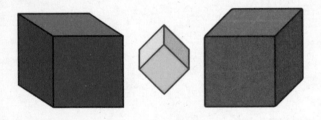

Count on from 5 to get the answer.

cube

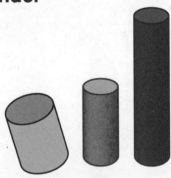

cylinder

data

Colors in the Bag								
Red	○	○	○					
Yellow	○	○	○	○	○	○	○	
Blue	○	○	○	○	○			

The **data** show how many of each color.

decade numbers

10, 20, 30, 40, 50, 60, 70, 80, 90

difference

$11 - 3 = 8$

$$\begin{array}{r} 11 \\ -\ 3 \\ \hline 8 \end{array}$$

difference →

digit

15 is a 2-**digit** number.

The 1 in 15 means 1 ten.

The 5 in 15 means 5 ones.

Dot Array

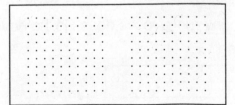

doubles

$$4 + 4 = 8$$

Both partners are the same.
They are **doubles**.

doubles minus 1

$7 + 7 = 14$, so

$7 + 6 = 13$, 1 less than 14.

doubles minus 2

$7 + 7 = 14$, so

$7 + 5 = 12$, 2 less than 14.

doubles plus 1

$6 + 6 = 12$, so

$6 + 7 = 13$, 1 more than 12.

doubles plus 2

$6 + 6 = 12$, so

$6 + 8 = 14$, 2 more than 12.

E

edge

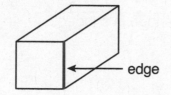

edge

equal shares

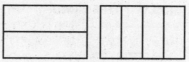

2 equal shares   4 equal shares

These show **equal shares.**

equal to (=)

$$4 + 4 = 8$$

4 plus 4 is **equal to** 8.

equation

Examples:

$$4 + 3 = 7 \qquad 7 = 4 + 3$$

$$9 - 5 = 4 \qquad 4 = 9 - 5$$

F

face

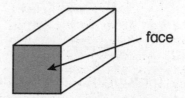

face

fewer

Eggs Laid This Month

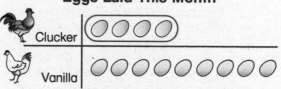

Clucker laid **fewer** eggs than Vanilla.

Glossary (continued)

fewest

Eggs Laid This Month

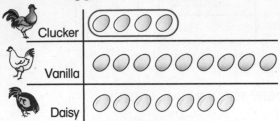

Clucker laid the **fewest** eggs.

fourth of

One **fourth of** the shape is shaded.

fourths

 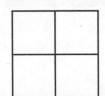

I whole   4 **fourths**, or 4 quarters

greater than (>)

34   >   25

34 is greater than 25.

grid

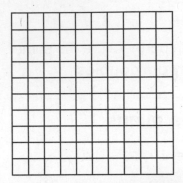

H

half-hour

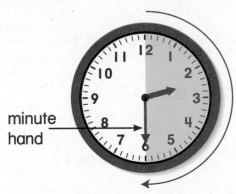

minute hand

A **half-hour** is 30 minutes.

half of

One **half of** the shape is shaded.

halves

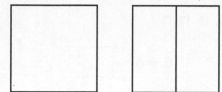

1 whole   2 **halves**

hexagon

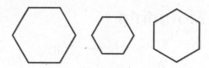

hour

hour hand

An **hour** is 60 minutes.

hundred

1	11	21	31	41	51	61	71	81	91
2	12	22	32	42	52	62	72	82	92
3	13	23	33	43	53	63	73	83	93
4	14	24	34	44	54	64	74	84	94
5	15	25	35	45	55	65	75	85	95
6	16	26	36	46	56	66	76	86	96
7	17	27	37	47	57	67	77	87	97
8	18	28	38	48	58	68	78	88	98
9	19	29	39	49	59	69	79	89	99
10	20	30	40	50	60	70	80	90	100

or

K

known partner

$5 + \boxed{} = 7$

5 is the **known partner**.

L

label

We see 9 fish.
5 are big. The others are small.
How many fish are small?

_____ fish

label

length

The **length** of this pencil is
6 paper clips.

less than (<)

45   <   46

45 is less than 46.

longer

The pencil is **longer** than the crayon.

longest

The pencil is **longest**.

M

make a ten

$8 + 6 =$ ☐

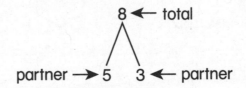

$10 + 4 = 14$,
so $8 + 6 = 14$.

Math Mountain

8 ← total

partner → 5   3 ← partner

measure

You can use paper clips to **measure** the
length of the pencil.

minus (−)

$8 - 3 = 5$ $\begin{array}{r} 8 \\ -3 \\ \hline 5 \end{array}$

8 **minus** 3 equals 5.

minute

There are 60 **minutes** in an hour.

more

Eggs Laid This Month

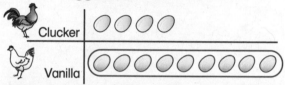

Vanilla laid **more** eggs than Clucker.

most

Eggs Laid This Month

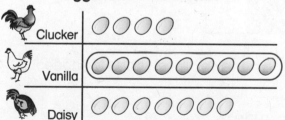

Vanilla laid the **most** eggs.

N

New Group Above Method

$$\begin{array}{r} \overset{1}{56} \\ + \ 28 \\ \hline 84 \end{array}$$ 6 + 8 = 14

The 1 new ten in 14 goes up to the tens place.

New Group Below Method

$$\begin{array}{r} 56 \\ + \ 28 \\ \hline 8\overset{1}{4} \end{array}$$ 6 + 8 = 14

The 1 new ten in 14 goes below in the tens place.

not equal to (≠)

6 ≠ 8

6 is **not equal to** 8.

number word

12

twelve ← number word

O

ones

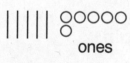

ones

56 has 6 **ones**.

order

You can change the **order** of the partners.

7 + 2 = 9

2 + 7 = 9

You can **order** objects by length.

1

2

3

P

partner

5 = 2 + 3

2 and 3 are **partners** of 5.
2 and 3 are 5-**partners**.

partner house

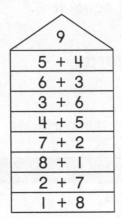

9
5 + 4
6 + 3
3 + 6
4 + 5
7 + 2
8 + 1
2 + 7
1 + 8

partner train

4-train

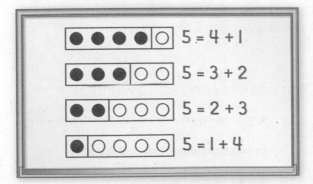

3 + 1   2 + 2   1 + 3

pattern

5 = 4 + 1
5 = 3 + 2
5 = 2 + 3
5 = 1 + 4

The partners of a number show a **pattern**.

plus (+)

3 + 2 = 5

$$\begin{array}{r} 3 \\ + 2 \\ \hline 5 \end{array}$$

3 **plus** 2 equals 5.

Proof Drawing

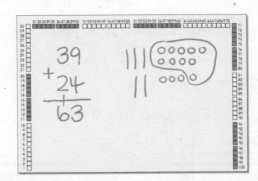

Q

quarter of

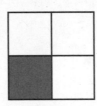

One **quarter of** the shape is shaded.

quarters

1 whole   4 **quarters**, or 4 fourths

rectangle

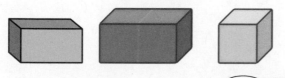

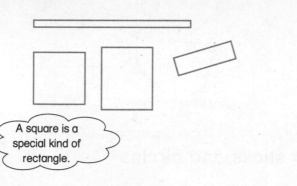

A square is a special kind of rectangle.

rectangular prism

A cube is a special kind of rectangular prism.

row

1	11	21	31	41	51	61	71	81	91
2	12	22	32	42	52	62	72	82	92
3	13	23	33	43	53	63	73	83	93
4	14	24	34	44	54	64	74	84	94
5	15	25	35	45	55	65	75	85	95
6	16	26	36	46	56	66	76	86	96
7	17	27	37	47	57	67	77	87	97
8	18	28	38	48	58	68	78	88	98
9	19	29	39	49	59	69	79	89	99
10	20	30	40	50	60	70	80	90	100

shapes

2-dimensional 3-dimensional

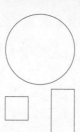 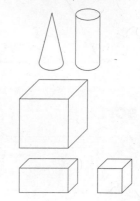

shorter

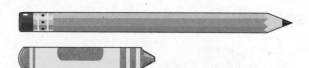

The crayon is **shorter** than the pencil.

shortest

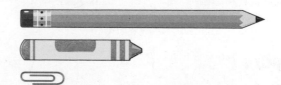

The paper clip is the **shortest**.

Show All Totals Method

$$
\begin{array}{r}
25 \\
+\ 48 \\
\hline
60 \\
13 \\
\hline
73
\end{array}
$$

side

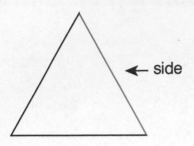

square corner

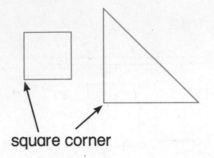

sort

You can **sort** the bugs into groups.

sphere

square

sticks and circles

I	○
II	│ ○
2I	││ ○
3I	│││ ○

subtract

8 − 3 = 5

subtraction story problem

8 flies are on a log.
6 are eaten by a frog.
How many flies are left?

switch the partners

7 + 2

2 + 7

T

teen number

11 12 13 14 15 16 17 18 19

teen numbers

teen total

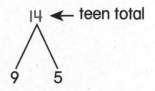

14 ← teen total

9   5

tens

||||| ○○○○○
       ○

tens

56 has 5 **tens**.

total

4 + 3 = 7

$$\begin{array}{r} 4 \\ + 3 \\ \hline 7 \end{array}$$

total →

trapezoid

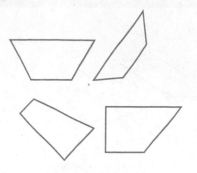

triangle

U

unknown partner

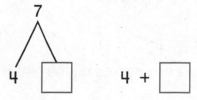

7

4

4 + ☐ = 7

unknown total

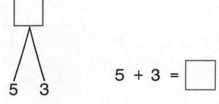

5   3

5 + 3 = ☐

© Houghton Mifflin Harcourt Publishing Company

V

vertex

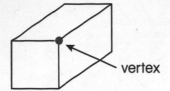

vertex

vertical form

$$6 \quad \quad 9$$
$$+3 \quad -3$$
$$\overline{9} \quad \overline{6}$$

Z

zero

There are **zero** apples on the plate.